P9-EDY-245

Gangs and Crime

CRIME, JUSTICE, AND PUNISHMENT

Gangs and Crime

Richard Worth

Austin Sarat, GENERAL EDITOR

CHELSEA HOUSE PUBLISHERS
Philadelphia

Frontispiece: *Members of a Crips set, Los Angeles*.

Chelsea House Publishers

Editor in Chief Sally Cheney
Director of Production Kim Shinners
Production Manager Pamela Loos
Art Director Sara Davis
Senior Editor John Ziff
Production Editor Diann Grasse
Cover Design Keith Trego

Layout by 21st Century Publishing and
Communications, Inc., New York, N.Y.

First Printing

1 3 5 7 9 8 6 4 2

The Chelsea House World Wide Web address is
http://www.chelseahouse.com

Library of Congress Cataloging-in-Publication Data
CIP applied for ISBN 0-7910-5767-4

Contents

CRIME, JUSTICE, AND PUNISHMENT

Fears and Fascinations:

An Introduction to Crime, Justice, and Punishment

By Austin Sarat

We live with crime and images of crime all around us. Crime evokes in most of us a deep aversion, a feeling of profound vulnerability, but it also evokes an equally deep fascination. Today, in major American cities the fear of crime is a major fact of life, some would say a disproportionate response to the realities of crime. Yet the fear of crime is real, palpable in the quickened steps and furtive glances of people walking down darkened streets. At the same time, we eagerly follow crime stories on television and in movies. We watch with a "who done it" curiosity, eager to see the illicit deed done, the investigation undertaken, the miscreant brought to justice and given his just deserts. On the streets the presence of crime is a reminder of our own vulnerability and the precariousness of our taken-for-granted rights and freedoms. On television and in the movies the crime story gives us a chance to probe our own darker motives, to ask "Is there a criminal within?" as well as to feel the collective satisfaction of seeing justice done.

Fear and fascination, these two poles of our engagement with crime, are, of course, only part of the story. Crime is, after all, a major social and legal problem, not just an issue of our individual psychology. Politicians today use our fear of, and fascination with, crime for political advantage. How we respond to crime, as well as to the political uses of the crime issue, tells us a lot about who we are as a people as well as what we value and what we tolerate. Is our response compassionate or severe? Do we seek to understand or to punish, to enact an angry vengeance or to rehabilitate and welcome the criminal back into our midst? The CRIME, JUSTICE, AND PUNISHMENT series is designed to explore these themes, to ask why we are fearful and fascinated, to probe the meanings and motivations of crimes and criminals and of our responses to them, and, finally, to ask what we can learn about ourselves and the society in which we live by examining our responses to crime.

Crime is always a challenge to the prevailing normative order and a test of the values and commitments of law-abiding people. It is sometimes a Raskolnikov-like act of defiance, an assertion of the unwillingness of some to live according to the rules of conduct laid out by organized society. In this sense, crime marks the limits of the law and reminds us of law's all-too-regular failures. Yet sometimes there is more desperation than defiance in criminal acts; sometimes they signal a deep pathology or need in the criminal. To confront crime is thus also to come face-to-face with the reality of social difference, of class privilege and extreme deprivation, of race and racism, of children neglected, abandoned, or abused whose response is to enact on others what they have experienced themselves. And occasionally crime, or what is labeled a criminal act, represents a call for justice, an appeal to a higher moral order against the inadequacies of existing law.

Figuring out the meaning of crime and the motivations of criminals and whether crime arises from defiance, desperation, or the appeal for justice is never an easy task. The motivations and meanings of crime are as varied as are the persons who engage in criminal conduct. They are as mysterious as any of the mysteries of the human soul. Yet the desire to know the secrets of crime and the criminal is a strong one, for in that knowledge may lie one step on the road to protection, if not an assurance of one's own personal safety. Nonetheless, as strong as that desire may be, there is no available technology that can allow us to know the whys of crime with much confidence, let alone a scientific certainty. We can, however, capture something about crime by studying the defiance, desperation, and quest for justice that may be associated with it. Books in the CRIME, JUSTICE, AND PUNISHMENT series will take up that challenge. They tell stories of crime and criminals, some famous, most not, some glamorous and exciting, most mundane and commonplace.

This series will, in addition, take a sober look at American criminal justice, at the procedures through which we investigate crimes and identify criminals, at the institutions in which innocence or guilt is determined. In these procedures and institutions we confront the thrill of the chase as well as the challenge of protecting the rights of those who defy our laws. It is through the efficiency and dedication of law enforcement that we might capture the criminal; it is in the rare instances of their corruption or brutality that we feel perhaps our deepest betrayal. Police, prosecutors, defense lawyers, judges, and jurors administer criminal justice and in their daily actions give substance to the guarantees of the Bill of Rights. What is an adversarial system of justice? How does it work? Why do we have it? Books in the CRIME, JUSTICE, AND PUNISHMENT series will examine the thrill of the chase as we seek to capture the criminal. They will also reveal the drama and majesty of the criminal trial as well as the day-to-day reality of a criminal justice system in which trials are the exception and negotiated pleas of guilty are the rule.

When the trial is over or the plea has been entered, when we have separated the innocent from the guilty, the moment of punishment has arrived. The injunction to punish the guilty, to respond to pain inflicted by inflicting pain, is as old as civilization itself. "An eye for an eye and a tooth for a tooth" is a biblical reminder that punishment must measure pain for pain. But our response to the criminal must be better than and different from the crime itself. The biblical admonition, along with the constitutional prohibition of "cruel and unusual punishment," signals that we seek to punish justly and to be just not only in the determination of who can and should be punished, but in how we punish as well. But neither reminder tells us what to do with the wrongdoer. Do we rape the rapist, or burn the home of the arsonist? Surely justice and decency say no. But, if not, then how can and should we punish? In a world in which punishment is neither identical to the crime nor an automatic response to it, choices must be made and we must make them. Books in the CRIME, JUSTICE, AND PUNISHMENT series will examine those choices and the practices, and politics, of punishment. How do we punish and why do we punish as we do? What can we learn about the rationality and appropriateness of today's responses to crime by examining our past and its responses? What works? Is there, and can there be, a just measure of pain?

CRIME, JUSTICE, AND PUNISHMENT brings together books on some of the great themes of human social life. The books in this series capture our fear and fascination with crime and examine our responses to it. They remind us of the deadly seriousness of these subjects. They bring together themes in law, literature, and popular culture to challenge us to think again, to think anew, about subjects that go to the heart of who we are and how we can and will live together.

*   *   *   *   *

The line between social activity and criminal activity is frequently quite blurred. While we may want to see crime as a radical departure from, and an abrupt break with, the bonds of sociability, in truth crime is often embedded in those very bonds. Doing crime builds networks. Doing crime establishes relationships. Gangs and gang activity are but one expression of these facts of social life.

Gangs and Crime effectively brings social science research and case examples together to produce a compelling account of the role of gangs in the world of crime. It shows how gangs arise, what roles they play in the lives of young people, and the kinds of law enforcement strategies that are used to combat gangs. It reminds us that gangs have a long and storied history in the United States. Young males especially have regularly come together and defined their masculinity through acts of violence. This book analyzes gangs from the outside, but also effectively explores the experiences and "pleasures" of gang membership. As such it reminds us that despite the best efforts of the police, it may be very difficult to break the linkage of gangs and crime.

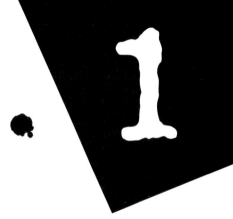

GANGS: A TERRIBLE FACT OF LIFE

In inner-city neighborhoods across the United States, ordinary citizens fear for their safety. The reason: street gangs. "I have never had the terror that I feel every day when I walk down the streets of Chicago," one resident of the Windy City revealed. "I have had my windows broken out. I have had guns pulled on me. I have been threatened." A resident of Lincoln, Nebraska, reported a similar experience: "This used to be a really nice neighborhood, but now you have to be afraid for your life." Lincoln has at least 23 different street gangs, whose members carry semiautomatic handguns, steal stereos and cellular phones, and have been implicated in drug dealing and theft rings.

But the problem of street gangs is by no means limited to America's cities. In a suburban area of Prince George's County, Maryland, for example, gang members bashed in the head of a 14-year-old girl. Her offense? She warned a friend that the gang was planning to kill him.

Members of a police antigang squad arrest two young suspects. Throughout much of the United States, street gangs are an unfortunate fact of life.

What, exactly, is a street gang? One expert defines it as "an organization of young people usually between their early teens and early twenties, which has a group name, claims a territory or neighborhood as its own, meets with its members on a regular basis, and has recognizable leadership . . . [and] its members regularly participate in activities that violate the law." Of course, this definition doesn't capture all the subtleties and variations of what is a rather complex social problem.

For instance, although members of street gangs are primarily in their teens and early twenties, the leaders of some gangs may be 10 or 20 years older. And while the teenage years are typically when most gang members get their start, some gangs have actively recruited kids as young as eight or nine. The shocking case of Robert "Yummy" Sandifer drove this home for many Americans. In 1994, Sandifer, age 11, was executed on a railroad underpass by members of his own Chicago gang. Earlier, he had killed a 14-year-old girl by mistake, drawing attention to the gang.

Although street gangs spring from—and claim as their own—a particular neighborhood or territory, they sometimes expand well beyond that area and create criminal links with cohorts all around the nation. During the late 1960s or early 1970s, Stanley "Tookie" Williams started a gang in Los Angeles called the Crips. By 1980 the gang boasted 30,000 members in Los Angeles County. And by the 1990s many Crips sets— separate, often loosely affiliated gangs using the Crips name—had sprung up. For example, the Los Angeles– based Fruittown Crips claims a neighborhood where the streets are named after different types of fruits.

The Crips did not remain in Los Angeles, however. Various sets have emerged across the country—each with its own leader, members, and territory. According to federal law enforcement agencies, the Crips are heavily involved in selling illegal drugs. They import large quantities of cocaine from abroad and manufacture

Chicago police remove the body of Robert "Yummy" Sandifer. In a case that shocked the nation, the 11-year-old was executed by members of his own gang.

crack in the United States. Affiliations among various Crips sets, as well as alliances with other organized-crime groups, have enabled the gang to find new markets for its drugs and expand its reach across the continent.

During the last quarter of the 20th century, street gangs as a whole steadily increased their power, reaching into cities and suburban communities across America. According to a study conducted by the U.S. Department of Justice's Office of Juvenile Justice and Delinquency Prevention (OJJDP), there were approximately 2,300 gangs with 98,000 members during the 1970s. These gangs were primarily located in large cities such as Los Angeles, Chicago, New York, and Detroit. The study reported that more than 40 percent of all arrests for violent crimes involved gang members.

By the early and mid-1990s, law enforcement statistics revealed much more extensive gang activity. In 1996 gang membership peaked at an estimated 846,000 individuals. As many as 31,000 gangs—more than 600 for each state—were active. According to one study, street gangs were present in 94 percent of all U.S. cities with populations greater than 100,000. Los Angeles alone had an estimated 950 gangs with more than 100,000 members. Street gangs had also spread to smaller cities. By 1992, 86 percent of smaller cities reported problems with gangs, and almost 100 cities with populations less than 10,000 had street gangs. Not even the smallest of towns could expect to be free from street gangs. Studies of rural areas in states such as Colorado, Iowa, Michigan, Montana, New Hampshire, South Carolina, and Texas implicated gangs in many serious crimes.

The situation became difficult to ignore at the national level, and federal law enforcement officials, along with members of the judiciary, called for action. "Gangs," Supreme Court justice Clarence Thomas declared, "fill the daily lives of many of our poorest and most vulnerable citizens with a terror . . . relegating them to the status of prisoners in their own homes." Thomas said that one man told him that he began carrying a meat cleaver to work because he was so afraid of the street gangs in his neighborhood.

Authorities noted that the rise in gang activity paralleled an increase in serious crimes committed by juveniles during the 1980s and early 1990s. The murder rate among juveniles more than doubled between 1987 and 1993. Robberies rose by 70 percent between 1988 and 1994, and aggravated assault increased by more than 120 percent during that period. While most experts concede that a host of factors influence crime rates, the connection between juvenile gangs and the rise in juvenile crime rates received much attention. In some instances strong evidence suggested that a correlation existed. For example, law enforcement authorities in Los Angeles attributed as many as 40 percent of the juvenile killings in their jurisdiction to gang disputes over drugs and turf.

During the last part of the 1990s, however, juvenile violence—and with it gang activity—began to decline. A survey published in 1999 by the National Youth Gang Center polled more than 1,000 police departments in cities and suburban areas. The number of police agencies reporting gang activity had declined by 5 percent from the number reporting such activity three years earlier, in 1996. The number of active gangs had fallen from 31,000 in 1996 to about 28,500 in 1999. And the number of estimated gang members had decreased to about 780,000 from 846,000.

In Los Angeles, an area of abundant gang activity, police reported 805 gang-related murders in 1995; by the following year this number had dropped to 200. Much of the decline may be attributable to an improved economy. When jobs are readily available, crime as a whole tends to drop. Nevertheless, gangs continue to be associated with violence and crime. About 89 percent of all juvenile crime, according to the National Youth Gang Center, is committed by gang members.

It's not just young men who are at risk, either. Although an estimated 92 percent of gang members are males between the ages of 15 and 24, females also join gangs. Often gang girls are associated with an established male gang, which may use them in support roles in various criminal activities (for example, as lookouts during drug sales). Sometimes, however, gang girls serve primarily as romantic partners for male gang members. In some gangs, the "jumping in," or initiation, rituals for girls involve having sex with many or all of the male gang members. Nevertheless, many female street gangs aren't associated with any male gang. Like their male

A gang couple, San Diego. Gang membership among girls is much lower than among boys, and although some girls belong to independent gangs, many are affiliated with male gangs.

counterparts, these independent groups maintain their own leadership hierarchies and rules for membership.

As a rule, female street gangs are much less likely than their male cohorts to become involved in violent crime, but that is by no means universally the case. For her book *8 Ball Chicks*, author Gini Sikes spent a year with girl gang members and uncovered many stories of violence. One girl named Coco, a member of the Grape Street Watts Crips in Los Angeles, supported herself through robbery. Once, when a girl owed her $100, Coco threatened her. "She said she wasn't going to pay me," Coco recalled. "So I shot into the house three times. I wouldn't really have hit her kids, but I got my money." Another girl Sikes interviewed broke into cars and accompanied male gang members when they entered enemy turf to fight a rival gang.

More than any other factor, violence characterizes gang life. In a survey, 50 percent of gang members reported using guns in assaults "often" or "sometimes." A study conducted for the Department of Justice in cities such as Denver and Cleveland showed that gang members are more likely to assault innocent citizens and commit murder than youth who do not belong to gangs. The study revealed that more than half of all gang members had committed drive-by shootings, which are unexpected, violent, random, and anonymous assaults on rival gang members from a moving car. Unfortunately, innocent people sometimes get killed in the crossfire.

But violence isn't all that gangs are up to. In the Cleveland study, gang members were found to be far more likely to sell drugs than young people who did not belong to gangs. Police in many jurisdictions report that most drugs sales involve street gangs, or at least gang members who work for organized crime groups controlled by adults. Representative Maxine Waters, a congresswoman from South Central Los Angeles, recently asserted that during the 1980s and 1990s, gangs like the Crips had sold "tons of cocaine" on the streets of L.A. "But not only did they bring the drugs in," Congresswoman Waters added, "they brought the guns along with them."

Law enforcement officials have attested to the accuracy of Congresswoman Waters's assessment. The illegal drug trade is tremendously lucrative, and gangs must always be prepared to fend off would-be rivals who hope to carve out some market share at their expense. Especially during the 1980s, when competition for the crack market was most intense, gangs armed themselves to the teeth. Not surprisingly, powerful firearms—9-mm pistols, semiautomatic rifles, sometimes even military-style automatic rifles—found their way into the hands of the drug wars' soldiers, who were often teenage gang members. Though the crack wars have largely subsided with the elimination of the weakest gangs and the entrenchment of the stronger and more ruthless ones, the firepower remains. Indeed, many experts have blamed high juvenile homicide rates primarily on the availability of guns, which is in part a residual effect of the arms race between rival drug-dealing gangs.

Although the drug trade generates enormous profits, that is not to say that selling drugs will put a lot of money in the pockets of an average gang member. In fact, economists at the University of Chicago and Harvard University who examined the financial benefits of selling drugs for gang members made some stunning findings. Most gang members in the study— the couriers, the lookouts, the low-level street dealers, the enforcers—were paid less than the current federal minimum wage. This was true even though these gang members constantly exposed themselves to the risk of arrest, serious injury, or even a sudden and violent death. Still, the lion's share of the drug profits went to the gang leaders, who could expect to earn $100,000 a year. Gang members were paid more money during a turf war—in which gangs battle to increase their territory, and thus their profits from the drug trade—because the risk of dying increased enormously at these times. Over a four-year period during a turf war, the study found, a gang member suffered on average two serious injuries and had a 25 percent chance of being killed.

If the pay for most gang members is low and the chance of dying relatively high, why would a kid become involved in these drug wars? According to the economists, the answer lies in the potential rewards: the gang members hope to survive and eventually become a gang leader, thereby being in a position to earn large amounts of money. It's a high-stakes gamble, but the potential payoff makes it worthwhile for some youths, especially those who don't think they have many other options for succeeding.

One young man took the bet, but never made it to gang leadership. By day, he was a teacher's aide in a local elementary school. But after school, unknown to the teachers or the principal, he was a member of a local street gang and sold drugs. Unfortunately, he irritated the members of a rival gang, who killed him in a drive-by shooting near the school.

This story shows that gangs aren't limited to neighborhoods. They have become an increasingly serious problem in our schools. For many years they were present in high schools; but gangs have also spread to middle and even elementary schools. A report issued jointly by the U.S. Departments of Justice and Education detailed the growth of gang activities in America's schools. According to the report, the number of students who said that gangs were in their schools had doubled between 1989 and 1995. Approximately 37 percent of all students reported that gangs existed in their schools. These gangs had a name, a recognized leader, and their own turf. They also wore clothing, such as shirts or jackets, indicating they were gang members. As in most cases, the gang members tended to hang out together in school as well as out, and they were known to commit acts of violence. The presence of a gang also meant that students were more likely to be seen carrying guns.

Indeed, about 38 percent of the students said that gang members had been involved in violence in their schools. And the more drugs there were available in the schools, the more likely that gangs were there selling them.

Students also reported that they were more likely to be victimized—for example, by having money stolen or by being physically attacked—when gangs were present. The Departments of Justice and Education study found that school-based gangs were more likely to operate in schools located in low-income urban neighborhoods where minority students, especially Hispanics and African Americans, attended classes.

According to recent reports, major gangs—including branches of the Crips—have also spread to the armed forces. These gangs actively try to enlist the teenage sons and daughters of military personnel. Like their counterparts in the civilian world, members of these gangs are involved in crimes ranging from the sale of illegal drugs to robbery and even murder.

Indian reservations are another place where gang activity is on the rise. According to the Bureau of Indian Affairs, there are over 500 Indian gangs with more than 6,000 members. The murder rate on one Navaho reservation is now higher than that in Chicago or Los Angeles. Indeed, the homicide rate on Indian reservations increased by 50 percent between 1992 and 1999, and the blame seems mostly to fall upon gangs. As one Navaho police official put it, "The murders went up when we started having gang problems."

As Indians leave reservations and go to the cities looking for work, some of them join gangs. If they return home, the gang affiliation returns with them and they recruit other members on the reservation. Other Indians join gangs if they are convicted of crimes and go to prison. Most of the gang-related crime on Indian reservations doesn't involve drugs or robberies. Instead, the gangs battle over territory and the prestige that comes with defeating a rival. As one expert explained, "The violence is real turf-oriented."

According to the Federal Bureau of Investigation, street gangs are becoming more sophisticated. Not only are gangs using more expensive weapons, the FBI notes,

but increasingly they are also communicating with each other on the Internet and adopting the savvy business practices that have enabled organized crime groups to reap vast profits.

This new sophistication and attention to money-making hasn't decreased the level of violence among street gangs, however. In fact, gang members have a 60 percent greater risk of suffering a violent death than do other young people. But the violence doesn't stop there. Innocent citizens also pay a heavy price, being victimized by drive-by killings, armed robbery, and the random violence that erupts between rival gangs when they battle over turf.

Gang violence has touched even remote areas of the United States. Here, a detective sergeant with the Salt River Police Department in Arizona stands outside a graffiti-covered house on an Indian reservation—the site of a gang murder.

A Brief
History
of Gangs

treet gangs are more prominent in the United States than other countries because we are a nation of immigrants. From the Irish toughs of 19th-century New York to the Southeast Asian drug runners of modern-day California, young men of the same ethnic background have banded together to preserve their cultural identities and protect themselves from discrimination. The gangs have also been a way to make money in an economy that offered their particular group few opportunities for advancement, which explains the rise of gangs among African Americans as well. Although blacks have been part of the American culture for centuries, they remain a racial minority plagued by disadvantage and discrimination.

Street gangs thrive particularly in areas of extreme social disorganization and family disintegration. This may be due, in part, to the fact that in neighborhoods in which adult crime is a problem, young people model the criminal attitudes and behaviors of their elders. Likewise, when a significant proportion of the adult male population is incarcerated—as is the case, for example, in some African-American communities—the informal social controls that men provide to moderate the behavior of adolescent youths are lost. In other words, in the absence of sufficient male authority figures, boys frequently turn to gangs. In addition, dysfunctional or broken families constitute a risk factor for juvenile gang membership. Experts usually attribute this to the youth's search for the attention, acceptance, and structure that are missing at home. (It should be noted that all of the above factors contribute not simply to gang membership but also to juvenile crime in general.)

More subtle forces have also been at work in the rise of American street gangs. Our society has always romanticized the outsider image of the gangster, possibly because this country began, after all, as a nation of outsiders willing to take risks and buck tradition. Even deadly gangsters such as Al Capone and Bonnie and Clyde have become heroes of American folklore. Their fictional counterparts in today's films are even more murderous. The solitary tough guy who operates outside the law, and for whom murder and destruction are the rule of the day, is a staple of American cinema. At the same time these characters are wreaking havoc on the big screen, young people are playing violent video games just outside the entrance to movie theaters. Whether we are comfortable admitting it or not, our society tacitly approves of violence.

"The unique American gang and its mad bloodletting has emerged in the fertile soil of a society that has in this past century developed violence into an art form," writes sociologist Lewis Yablonsky, one of the country's foremost experts on gangs. So gangs have offered not only a source of safety for America's outsiders but also a source of power. For young people who are poor, undereducated, and without access to decent jobs, gangs have been a seductive alternative to boredom

An engraving of three Bowery Boys, New York City. The Bowery Boys gang was one of the first in the United States, arising just after the Revolutionary War.

and hopelessness. They are a way to make money and achieve status. Gangs proudly promote values, even killing and stealing, that are in tantalizing opposition to the dominant values of a rejecting society.

The earliest identified American gangs formed just after the Revolutionary War among the poorer classes in the emerging cities. They sported names like Smith's Vly gang, the Bowery Boys, the Long Ridge Boys, and the Fly Boys. Their members were the sons of western European settlers, and they came together for recreation as much as protection and modest financial gain.

As the growing nation's cities teemed with immigrant factory workers during the Industrial Revolution of the 19th century, gangs thrived—especially amid rampant municipal corruption. Irish, Jewish, and Italian gang members burned ballot boxes on behalf of their favored candidates, and plundered homes and stores for their own benefit, with little fear of police interference.

Growing competition for jobs, meanwhile, contributed to gang rivalry and territorialism. Irish immigrants are credited with forming the first truly criminal gangs in New York City in the early 1800s. The first Irish gang with a recognized leader was the Forty Thieves, organized by Edward Coleman in 1826. Irish gangs also formed in Boston in response to the ethnic and economic discrimination by the Brahmin bluebloods, the New England social elite who controlled jobs and paid unfairly low wages. After the Civil War, with increased immigration from Europe and the migration of newly freed southern slaves to northern urban centers, gang membership continued to swell.

During the Roaring Twenties, Prohibition—when the importation, manufacture, and sale of alcohol was prohibited by the 18th Amendment to the U.S. Constitution—spurred young gang members to seek their fortunes and forge fearsome reputations by selling illegal liquor. The youth gangs of New York City's Lower East Side, the heart of immigrant communities, imitated adult bootleggers. They adopted names like the Dusters, the Pug Uglies, the Dead Rabbits, and Five Points—monikers that reflected both their home neighborhood and the tough image they hoped to project. In Yablonsky's view, the bootlegging of the 1920s set the stage for today's illegal drug dealing and drive-by shootings. In fact, he credits Al Capone with developing the drive-by technique of mercilessly shooting a rival and quickly escaping by car. Capone was among several legendary gangsters who came of age during this period and got his start in an ethnic-based youth gang. Lucky Luciano was one of Capone's fellow Italian gangsters, while Meyer Lansky and Bugsy Siegel graduated from Jewish street gangs and went on to become two of the most prominent underworld figures in the United States.

Polish-American youths also formed gangs, including one called the Murderers, near the stockyards of Chicago. With its own bustling immigrant communities, Chicago became the focus of a landmark 1928 study of street gangs by sociologist Frederic Thrasher, which documented more than 1,000 "kid gangs" drawn from several ethnic groups. Famed Mafia boss Sam Giancana was one kid gang alumnus. So were brothers Jimmy and Frank Ragen, who graduated from their German-Irish street gang to win public office in Chicago—even while continuing to run illegal gambling rings. Even in these relatively innocent times, Thrasher concluded that "gangs exist to fill the void of social disorganization in lower-class communities."

As the Murderers' name suggests, violence was undoubtedly a part of the young gangster's life, but it was largely limited to fist-fighting and the wielding of baseball bats and knives. Large-scale killing rampages with guns had yet to begin. These early-20th-century gangs, despite their criminal activity, also remained connected to their neighborhood's religious, social, and political groups. So they weren't entirely isolated from the legitimate world (although in many instances, young gangsters often served as henchmen for corrupt politicians and businessmen).

The early Chicano gangs of East Los Angeles were particularly respectful of neighborhood elders and families; they followed strict codes of ethics that forbade involving innocent bystanders in intergang rivalry. East Los Angeles developed into a Chicano enclave in the 1920s, when poor Mexican migrants, who had gathered in the heart of L.A.'s Civic Center neighborhood, near an old mission, were driven across the Los Angeles River by new development. They settled in scrubby hillsides and canyons reminiscent of their homeland and set up shacks along unpaved roads. "It was natural for the young men of each barrio [neighborhood] to congregate to boast of audacious acts," a *Los Angeles Times* story recalled.

"In Mexico, it's expected that the young bucks will hang around and do daring, aggressive things," anthropologist James Diego Vigil told the *Los Angeles Times*. "It's a cohorting tradition." The Latin culture of machismo also expressed itself in the stylish dress of these early Chicano gangs, who favored the tapered pants and broad shoulders of the so-called zoot suits when they went out on the town. The famed Zoot Suit Riots of 1943, in which Mexican-American youths and white soldiers clashed near L.A.'s military bases, took their name from the popular clothes that were closely associated with Chicano gangs.

The riots also underscored the rising bigotry of the time and place. This was during World War II, a xenophobic era when American citizens of Japanese descent were rounded up throughout Southern California and sent to prison camps because of fear they would commit treason simply because the United States was at war with Japan. Although Mexico played no role in the war, many white Americans were nonetheless suspicious of anyone different from themselves. The Sleepy Lagoon murder case of 1942, a high-profile crime for which several Chicano teenagers were arrested and tried, also intensified mistrust between Mexican-Americans and whites and may have indirectly contributed to the Chicano gang subculture, where youths facing discrimination could find solace among their peers. One of the earliest Chicano gangs in East Los Angeles, the White Fence gang, took its name from a local church and formed in the 1940s to protect children who were being bullied by outsiders. It was one of the first Chicano gangs to use chains, and later guns, as weapons.

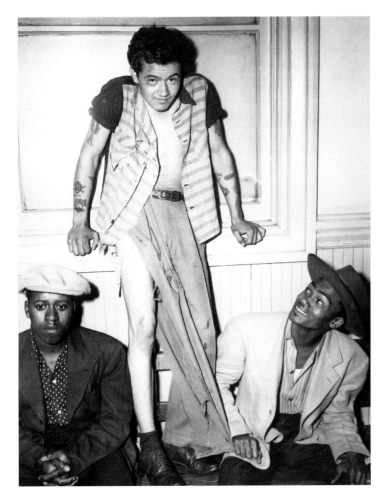

Bruised, his clothes torn, a Mexican-American participant in the so-called Zoot Suit Riots stands between two African Americans, Los Angeles, July 8, 1943.

On the East Coast, especially New York, the arrival of more than half a million Puerto Ricans between 1941 and 1945 gave rise to the Hispanic gangs immortalized in the musical *West Side Story*. This large influx of immigrants in such a short time was allowed by U.S. immigration laws because America was suffering from a labor shortage during World War II: workers were needed to replace the soldiers, sailors, and airmen fighting overseas. Still, the sheer numbers of arriving Puerto Ricans, and American disdain for their "foreign" culture, set the stage for a new wave of gangs. The resulting gang activity only ratcheted up the prejudice against Puerto Ricans, leading to more reasons for young Puerto Ricans to join gangs.

Guns were still rare even into the 1950s, and many gangsters of the time armed themselves with knives and homemade "zip guns." These highly unreliable weapons had metal pipes for barrels, wooden handles, and bunches of heavy elastic bands to provide shooting power. A bullet fired from a zip gun could just as easily hit the shooter as the intended victim, according to Yablonsky, who worked with gangs in New York during this period. Fighting between gangs at this time was called "rumbling," and some of the more prominent gangs included the white Jesters and their black and Puerto Rican rivals, the Egyptian Kings.

Despite their lack of sophisticated firepower, New York gangs entered a new level of violence in this period, targeting some victims for no particular reason and, in some instances, just to blow off steam. In the musical *West Side Story*, a modern retelling of William Shakespeare's *Romeo and Juliet*, Polish-American Tony, a leader of the Sharks, is killed by rivals in the Puerto Rican Jets because of his love affair with Maria. The real West Side Story, according to Yablonsky, who became a consultant on the case, involved the beating and stabbing death of a 15-year-old white boy crippled by polio. The victim, Michael Farmer, was killed on July 30, 1957, as he walked a friend home through Manhattan's Highbridge Park, near West 130th Street. Members of the Egyptian Kings, who were later tried for the murder, said they were bored and itching for a fight when Farmer and his friend happened to cross their path. The friend was also beaten but managed to hail a cab to a nearby emergency room and alert the police. The Michael Farmer killing was significant because it signaled the arrival of gratuitous violence among young gangsters and a complete forsaking of sacred values. Even Chicano gangs, once so loyal to their

native traditions, began cutting those ties during the social unrest of the 1960s.

Toward the end of the 20th century, "Cholos," as the Chicano gangsters sometimes called themselves, stopped speaking Spanish and began using and dealing drugs, despite the disapproval of the Catholic Church. They listened to hard rock instead of Latin music and affected a hippie style, calling themselves Stoners instead of Cholos. Some even began wearing their hair long and wearing jeans instead of the neatly pressed khaki pants and white T-shirts that had replaced zoot suits as the uniform of choice. California's Latino gangs changed even more during the 1980s following a huge influx of immigrants from war-torn Central America.

Scene from the 1961 film version of West Side Story, *whose plot concerned the tragic love affair between a Polish-American gang member and a Puerto Rican girl. The case that apparently inspired* West Side Story *was much less romantic: black gang members beat to death a white boy crippled with polio because they were bored.*

As thousands of teenage and preteen émigrés vied for acceptance on the arid streets of Los Angeles, they were willing to commit crazed acts to win their peers' respect. The advent of crack cocaine, a highly addictive and inexpensive form of the drug, in America's big cities only intensified the reckless and ruthless behavior.

The counterculture and class-consciousness of the 1960s not only changed Southern California's Cholos but also spawned new Los Angeles gangs in poor black neighborhoods south of the Hollywood Freeway, far from the sparkling waters of Malibu or manicured lawns of Beverly Hills. There the notorious Crips formed, adopting blue for their color and a complicated system of hand signals and tattoos to identify fellow members. The rival Pirus established themselves in nearby Compton, a predominantly black working-class town just south of L.A. The Pirus, named after Compton's West Piru Street, eventually became known as the Bloods because they wore the color red, and they were the only gang powerful enough to stand up to the Crips. Both gangs became so big that they actually comprised many mini-gangs, or sets, each representing different neighborhoods. The Crips, for example, included the Kitchen Crips, 5 Deuce Crips, and Rollin' 20 Crips, to name but a few.

Large and formidable black gangs also took root in Chicago during the 1960s, at a time when the confusing rules of the federal government's still-new welfare system had started to chip away at traditionally close-knit African-American families. (Only single mothers were entitled to benefits such as food stamps, for example, which prompted many poor couples to separate and many young women to have children out of wedlock.) Lingering prejudice and the lack of any affirmative action programs at the time made it extremely difficult for young African Americans to enter college or pursue any kind of white-collar job. Crime, including selling drugs, was a tempting way to make some money without having to kowtow to whites.

On Chicago's industrial South Side, drug dealer David Barksdale formed the Black Gangster Disciples, which he ran until he was murdered in 1974. Jeff Fort, who would end up receiving a prison sentence of 150 to 200 years for the murder of a rival, similarly formed the Blackstone Rangers. Throughout the 1960s, the Rangers and the Disciples carried out the bloodiest street fights on record in the city of Chicago. Why were young black men (not to mention Chicanos) killing each other like this instead of fighting the bigger, more righteous battle for civil rights that took place during the 1960s and 1970s? Many experts have come to view

Members of the Blackstone Rangers en route to a "peace conference" with the Black Gangster Disciples, Chicago, 1968. Throughout the 1960s, the two African-American gangs carried on a bloody war in the streets of the Windy City.

gang battles as an expression of self-hatred and, ultimately, a form of suicide—ideas to be explored more thoroughly in the next chapter.

Police have found that Asian gangsters similarly tend to prey on Asians, especially in the home-invasion robberies that became the trademark crime of young Southeast Asian gangsters during the 1980s and 1990s. In a home-invasion robbery, a band of well-organized thieves will force their way into a house or apartment, terrorize its occupants, and make off with as much cash and valuables as possible. Home-invasion robberies escalated across the United States after the fall of Saigon in 1975, when thousands of refugees from Vietnam, Laos, and Cambodia came to the United States to escape political persecution. Alienated teenage immigrants who joined gangs knew that many Southeast Asian families mistrusted banks and kept their savings at home. They also knew and exploited the fact that many Southeast Asian immigrants mistrusted authority after their experiences in their home countries, and were not likely to cooperate with the police. As a result, crimes perpetrated by Asian gangs proved hard to investigate and even harder to prosecute because of victims' reluctance to testify in court.

Another group frequently targeted by Southeast Asian gangs were Hmong families, the descendants of ethnic Chinese who migrated to the mountains of Vietnam, Laos, and Thailand in the 18th century. An ethnic minority back home, the Hmong once again found themselves victims of discrimination in the United States and demonstrated how gangs can perpetuate native traditions and pecking orders in a new land.

Asian gangs first appeared in the United States as early as the 1800s, when droves of Chinese laborers built the transcontinental railroad and settled into large enclaves in San Francisco and Chicago. Vietnamese gangs today often carry out the heavy work for more senior Chinese gangs. And some Asian gangs in

Chicago, meanwhile, maintain close ties to the Triads, a secret criminal society dating back to 17th-century China, where it formed to oppose dynastic rule.

These days, however, ethnicity seems to be taking a backseat to sheer size, firepower, and the ability to generate cash. As Yablonsky notes, gangs today serve more as an entry point into crime than a source of identity. The Los Angeles–based 18th Street gang, originally Chicano, has evolved into a sprawling, panethnic group with branches throughout the American West and across the Mexican border in Tijuana. Its incarcerated members constitute the largest bloc in California's juvenile justice system. In Los Angeles County alone, it has been linked to 150 murders between 1985 and 1995. The 18th Street gang recruits members from whatever recent group of immigrants is fresh and available, regardless of race or borders, because those are the people most likely to be struggling to make ends meet. And it targets recent immigrants as its victims, knowing they are less likely to report the crimes.

As our culture changes, so too do the gangs, and their reasons for existing also evolve. "Not only do gangs change," sociologist William Sanders has written, "but so too does what society considers gang behavior."

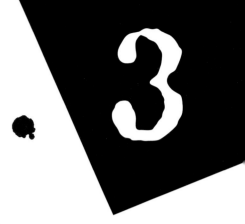

DEATH WISH: THE GANGSTER'S EMPTY WORLD

Gangs may have started as informal support groups for ethnic minorities, but today their unprecedented violence overshadows any other purpose. As crime rates confirm, gangsters are more antisocial and ruthless than ever before. More often than not, they victimize members of their own community. Experts seem to agree that hard-core gangsters are sociopaths, or emotionally warped people who feel so little connection to others that they are able to block out reality and the grave consequences of their actions. (Gang members whose consciences prevent them from blocking out their acts of violence against others won't advance in a gang and will generally drop out.)

Sociopaths are what psychologists call egocentric, meaning that they think only about themselves and their own needs. We are all concerned about our own well-being and take steps necessary to keep ourselves safe and happy. But sociopaths are self-absorbed in

According to some sociologists—as well as former gangbangers—the violence gang members enact on rivals often stems from self-hatred.

the extreme. They have limited social consciences. Like very young children, they are unable to put off immediate gratification for future goals. They are persistent liars, often to the point where they can no longer recognize the difference between their lies and the truth. All these characteristics of sociopaths, as sociologist Lewis Yablonsky has noted, perfectly match the behavior of most hard-core gangsters.

What makes a sociopathic gangster? Most grow up around violence, become inured to it, and know no other way of life. They tend to have absentee fathers, often fathers who are themselves convicted criminals and serving prison sentences. They frequently have overworked, stressed-out single mothers who may be physically and emotionally abusive themselves. Often a stepfather or other older male has beaten or sexually abused them. They live in neighborhoods where violent crime is commonplace. There is little joy or affection in these impoverished homes, no adult to set a consistent example of concern for others. "A child can't learn to be compassionate if he never sees any examples of caring in his crucial early years," Yablonsky writes.

Many gangsters today are the sons (and daughters) of alcoholics and drug addicts. They may have been born addicted to illegal drugs because their mother used drugs while she was pregnant. Or they may suffer from fetal alcohol syndrome, the permanent brain damage and learning disabilities that occur when mothers drink alcohol heavily during pregnancy. But even if they were born chemically free of drugs or alcohol, gangsters who grew up with substance-abusing elders probably had no one to take care of them on a regular basis. Substance-abusing parents are so consumed by feeding their own habits that they are unable to fulfill the most basic parental tasks. They don't go grocery shopping and prepare nutritious meals. They let laundry pile up. They don't

At the time this photo was taken, Lewis Morales (left) was 28 and the leader of New York's Sex Survivors gang. In violent street gangs, hard-core, sociopathic individuals tend to be the ones who remain long enough to assume leadership positions, and they often serve as mentors to younger members.

help their children with their homework or read to them; they don't organize constructive after-school activities; they don't even keep track of where their children are. "The child who cannot count on its own parents begins to become egocentric and therefore sociopathic in its behavior," eminent child psychologist Marshall Chirkas has written.

Neglect often combines with abuse, which further erodes a child's self-esteem. So gangs become a substitute family for youngsters who have no loving adult role model at home, especially a male role model. Just as Peter Pan led his Lost Boys on their adventures, so the older, hardened gangsters in a set become the leaders and teachers for these abandoned and abused kids. In his memoir, *Monster: The Autobiography of an L.A. Gang Member*, convicted killer Sanyika Shakur describes his sponsor in the notorious Eight Trays as both a coach-like figure and what he calls a general-father. Shakur was estranged from his own father, who he says had mistreated him, and was being raised with five siblings by his single mother. "Tray Ball became my mentor, friend, confidant, and closest comrade," Shakur writes. "He allowed me acts of aggression that made my name soar with alarming effects."

The loosely knit cadre of thieves, drug dealers, and killers becomes the closest thing to family structure young gangsters ever know. Bragging about being tough, acting macho, and then carrying out acts of violence compensates for the gangster's lack of self-esteem. Bragging usually involves at least some measure of exaggeration, and gangsters' exploits are often rooted in fantasy, Yablonsky and others have found. The violence is very real, but the rationale for these assaults is often trumped up or stems from slights so petty (or innocent) they seem incomprehensible to a rational person.

Early in *Monster*, whose title stems from the author's gang nickname, Shakur describes a potentially deadly gun battle that pitted himself and his brothers against the manager of a South Los Angeles hot-dog stand. Shakur says he opened fire directly into the fast-food restaurant because Eric, the manager, had had the audacity to ask Shakur's younger brother to pick up some paper wrappings he and a friend left at an outdoor table. Not only might the perpetrators of this meaningless exchange of gunfire have been killed, but so might have customers or passersby at the busy intersection of Florence and Normandie (not coincidentally, where the 1992 Los Angeles riots began). Was Shakur really that incensed over his brother's treatment, or was it just an excuse to be aggressive?

"Many murders characterized as gang related may have very little connection to gang retaliation and more to do with a disturbed sociopath's paranoia," Yablonsky writes. "The murderer's self-identification as a gang member gives the emotionally disturbed killer a cloak of immunity from being considered just plain crazy."

A similar sense of unreality extends to gangsters' sexual relationships, Yablonsky explains. Many young gang members emulate adult criminals in the simplistic view of women as either whores and bitches or saints. Often, gangsters will idealize girl-friends as sacred virgins—and threaten anyone who claims otherwise. This sort of denial can also be seen in prisons, where incarcerated gangsters (as well as other prisoners) regularly take part in homosexual liaisons both for pleasure and for punishment. Sodomy is the preferred form of punishment for an errant gang member, and oral sex is often demanded of subordinates. Yet gangsters officially disdain homosexuality and refuse to acknowledge either sodomy or the receiving of oral sex as an act of homosexuality on their part.

Some experts believe that, like most hate-mongers, gangsters really hate themselves. How else, these experts ask, can we explain their willingness to place themselves in the line of fire, either from other gang-sters or the police, day after day? Law-enforcement officers have a special phrase for situations in which a suspected criminal refuses to surrender and acts so recklessly that the police have no choice but to shoot. It's called "suicide by cop," or allowing yourself to be killed by officers because you cannot manage to kill yourself but have no desire to live. In the case of these tragic young sociopaths, the syndrome might be called "suicide by gangbanging."

When gangsters turn their guns on fellow Chicanos, African Americans, or Southeast Asians, their violence—in the view of some experts—reflects self-hatred on a massive scale and becomes a form of cultural genocide. While the idea is by no means universally accepted, Yablonsky, for example, has speculated that intraethnic violence stems from a hidden fear to directly take on the larger society's power structure. He compares it with family members venting their anger on one another instead of the teachers or bosses who are really upsetting them because, in the end, it's the safer thing to do.

One self-reflective Los Angeles gangster, Crips cofounder Stanley "Tookie" Williams, has described gang violence as a misguided attempt at self-purification by loathing members of a stereotyped race. "An individual who has been spoon-fed so many derogatory images of his race will, after a period of time, start to believe those images," Williams said in a *Los Angeles Times* interview. "And when an individual gets to believing such things, that individual gets to believing, 'Well, hell, if it's true, then I must be just as disgusting as those images that are being depicted.' So you end up lashing out at the individuals (other gang members) that you consider to be part of those stereotypes. In desperation, you're trying to obliterate that negative image to rid yourself of this self-hate monster that subconsciously stalks you. In a sense, you're trying to purify yourself, your environment, your race."

Williams, on death row at San Quentin Prison for murder, condemned urban violence and urged rival gangsters to reach a peace treaty at an unusual gangster summit meeting in Los Angeles in 1993. Speaking in a videotaped message that was played for the gathering, Williams was cheered by more than 400 gangsters in attendance. Later, during a *Los Angeles Times* interview, he said he was finally able to overcome his own self-loathing by immersing himself in learning while in prison and taking pride in small but significant accomplishments like being able to read and speak well. "I've been studying a lot since I've been in prison—economics, politics, black history, math, English, philosophy, psychology. And what I've learned has taught me to appeal to logic. If something's counterproductive, I don't want to have anything to do with it."

Williams was 41 years old at the time of the interview and had the benefit of maturity. Aspiring gangsters still in their teens or even preteens find it far more romantic to earn kudos by working their way up the gang ladder and committing gruesome acts of violence to win the approval of their peers. Violence becomes "an easy, quick, almost magical way of achieving power and prestige," says Yablonsky, adding that "any guilt is minimized by the gang's approval."

Gangs usually have a hierarchy led by the oldest, most experienced, most ruthless Original Gangsters, or OG's, at the top and served by an army of eager young recruits, or Wannabes, at the bottom. In between are the Veterans—or G's. OG's, who may be in their twenties or thirties, rarely carry out hits, thefts, or risky drug deals themselves, instead assigning these dangerous tasks to newcomers as young as 9 or 10 years old who are trying to forge their own reputations. Sometimes gangs are multigenerational, with both parents and children as members.

Wannabes often act as mules, or the subservient workers who transport drugs on the street and expose themselves not only to physical danger but to arrest. Drug use among gangsters themselves varies from one group to another. Almost all use marijuana and alcohol as a way to socialize, but some sociologists have found that Chicano gangsters tend to use hard drugs more than African-American gangsters because "kicking back," or partying with friends in the neighborhood, is a bigger part of their subculture.

African-American gangsters, as a rule, are more interested in making money and treat their drug-dealing more seriously. So ambitious Wannabes or G's in black gangs know not to overuse drugs themselves because getting addicted will hinder their effectiveness within the organization; they'll be viewed as screw-ups who cannot be counted on. And errant underlings are punished by anything from severe beatings to execution. Yablonsky has found that less sociopathic youths become only marginal gangsters, while the core gangsters in any group are the most severely sociopathic.

Just like any subculture, gangbanging has its own vocabulary. "Jumping in," or the gang initiation rite, usually involves both withstanding a beating and carrying out an act of violence. "Putting in work" means carrying out crimes and killings to earn credit within the gang. Having "heart" means having the guts to pull the trigger or commit some other violent act. "Smoking" someone means killing him, and a "wall up" murder means shooting someone execution style or at point-blank range. But for all the harm gangbanging does, and all the publicity it has generated in recent years, the main activity of gangsters is simply kicking back—cutting school, hanging out, getting high. The reality of gang life is that it is often quite boring: most gangsters have no place to go, no jobs to succeed in, no future to plan for.

"What do gangsters do? How do they spend their time?" one sociologist has asked. "Offhand, I can think of few categories of people who are less exciting to observe than gang members simply because, by and large, they just stand around and do nothing!"

Violence, then, becomes a thrill that jump-starts the emotional battery of a sociopathic individual and cements the bond of his sociopathic group. Unfortunately, violence tends to breed only more violence because its perpetrators become used to it. Like

addicts, Yablonsky has found, they need "increasingly heavier doses of bizarre and extreme violent behavior" to achieve the thrill. Seen in this light, then, turf wars are not only a way to increase gang territory, but also an excuse for acting out personal rage and feeding the habit of violence.

The toll of this self-destructive behavior has perhaps no more tragic symbol than Rancho Los

"Jumping in," or initiation into a gang, typically involves sustaining a beating from the other members of the gang and committing a (usually violent) crime. Here, members of Dallas's Low-Down Posse initiate a newcomer.

A fate shared by many gangbangers: 22-year-old Javier Francisco Ovando, seen here with his lawyers and his daughter, was paralyzed after being shot.

Amigos Medical Center near Los Angeles. A rehabilitative hospital that specializes in spinal-cord injuries, Rancho Los Amigos was once dominated by polio patients and car-accident victims relearning how to walk. Today its beds are filled with the survivors of gang shootings; as many as 100 are admitted a year. Some of the young men are not only paralyzed from the waist down, but were also rendered quadriplegic. They require the help of a machine to breathe, and the assistance of a human aide to eat, bathe, and use the bathroom. With little else to cling to except their reputations, many still drape their gang's colors on their beds and defend their gang's honor from their wheelchairs.

HOMICIDE
INFORMATION

KENNETH SORELL WILLIAMS
AKA: *BOOBIE; BLACK BOY; HI-TECH; SOREL WILLIAMS*
DOB: 9/18/70 - HEIGHT: 5'10" - WEIGHT: 160
GUNSHOT WOUND SCAR ON ABDOMEN

Williams is wanted for questioning in regard to multiple homicides. He has Open Warran
for Armed Robbery (F97-15879), Resisting Arrest (M97-20084), and has been indicted b
a Federal Grand Jury in the Southern District of Florida for Possession of a Firearm By
Convicted Felon (98-0280-8-CR-GOLD)and Conspiracy to Traffic in Cocaine. Williams ha
served prison time for Murder. He should be considered armed and extremely dangerou
If located, IMMEDIATELY CONTACT **MDPD HOMICIDE (305) 471-2400**

CRIMESTOPPERS OF DADE COUNTY, INC,
471-TIPS (471-8477)
ALL CALLERS REMAIN COMPLETELY ANONYMOUS -
*** $31,000 REWARD***

Gangs and Their Crimes

uring the 1990s, the FBI investigated the Grape Street Crips, which operated in Los Angeles. In 1995 investigators wiretapped the telephones of the gang's leaders and discovered that they were involved in a wide-ranging drug ring that operated in numerous cities in addition to Los Angeles, including Cleveland, Memphis, and Minneapolis. The gang also had links to a Mexican drug cartel that supplied the Crips with cocaine to sell on the streets. In May 1996, an FBI sting operation led to the arrest of 22 members of the Grape Street Crips. Large quantities of cocaine, as well as almost $500,000 in cash, were also seized.

A wanted poster for Kenneth Williams, leader of Miami's Boobie Boys gang. Law enforcement officials suspected the Boobie Boys of some three dozen murders over an eight-year span.

The wide reach, significant wealth, and formidable power of the Grape Street Crips is by no means unique among American gangs. According to the National Drug Intelligence Center, gangs affiliated with the Crips currently operate in 42

states. Chicago-based gangs such as the Black Gangster Disciples and the Almighty Latin Kings have
sets in 35 states. In addition, Hispanic gangs, like
Mara Salvatrucha and the 18th Street gang, are
currently operating in 41 states. Asian gangs, meanwhile, have penetrated more than 80 percent of the
United States.

On a national level, the sale of illegal drugs
constitutes the single most lucrative illegal activity
for gangs. Locally, however, gang members commit a
wide variety of crimes for money or simply to
increase their stature among their cohorts. One of
the most common types of gang crime is called
jacking, or robbery—and frequently the level of
violence used is excessive. Jacking is primarily a
crime of opportunity; it is aimed at individuals
foolish enough to wander onto the gang's turf. Gang
members usually mark their turf with graffiti drawn
on the walls of buildings and street signs.

"A white male was walking down the street when
a West Coast Crip approached and asked if he were
new to the area," a law-enforcement source said
in describing a typical jacking. "After the initial
contact, he started pushing him toward a vacant lot.
A second gang member then helped the first one get
the victim into the lot where seven other Crips
joined in beating and robbing the victim." Most
jackings involve several gang members who literally
"gang up" on their victim.

Gangs also make money by preying on businesses.
They rob stores and gas stations, assault and rob cab
drivers, and engage in shoplifting.

A favorite criminal variation, called "protection,"
is a kind of extortion technique. Gang members
approach a store or business owner and demand a
monthly sum—protection money. In return, they
promise not to interfere with the business and, in
some cases, actually to safeguard it from other

criminals. Businesspeople who refuse to pay risk being assaulted, robbed, or even killed, or having their store burned. Confronted with the threats, many store owners reluctantly pay out the protection money. Others whose establishments are in high-crime areas may convince themselves that the gang's assurances of protection from other criminals make paying the monthly sum a worthwhile investment, though just how vigilant gang members will be in this regard is uncertain.

Some gangbangers even shake down children on their way to elementary school. Under the threat of bodily injury, these children are forced to hand over their lunch money.

Not all gang violence against innocent members of the public has an economic motivation, however. In 1997, for example, at least 135 New Yorkers had their faces slashed by youthful assailants in random attacks on the streets. The perpetrators turned out to be Bloods; the attacks, initiation rites. To become full-fledged members of the gang, aspiring Bloods had to slash a stranger's face.

Some of the Bloods arrested for these slashings may have brought their violent tendencies to New York City's jails. According to one report, Bloods were responsible for more than half of the stabbings and slashings behind bars during 1997. Crips are also found in high numbers in New York prisons, where they have battled another gang, the Latin Kings, for dominance.

The Kings, a Hispanic gang, emerged as a force at New York's notorious Rikers Island jail. According to one report, they are among the fastest-growing gangs in New York City, recruiting members as young as eight years old. The Kings also have a significant presence in Connecticut, New Jersey, Illinois, Indiana, and Florida. Members wear black and gold clothing and sport tattoos such as a five-pointed

Cell blocks at Stateville Correctional Center, Crest Hill, Illinois. Gang affiliations—and rivalries—continue behind bars, and over the years American prisons and jails have witnessed a great deal of gang-related violence.

crown, five dots, or a five-pointed star. The Kings are heavily involved in drug trafficking, protection, and illegal weapons sales.

Gang violence often erupts when rivals, such as the Kings and the Crips, battle each other over turf. If someone from a rival gang is found on another gang's turf, he risks being beaten up or even killed. If they know that incursions on another gang's turf will be met with such a strong reaction, why do gang members still make such incursions? In some cases, more than just neighborhood pride is at stake. Rival gangs may do battle to take over turf—or defend their own—because it provides a lucrative market for selling drugs. During the 1990s, for instance, a Jamaican gang tried to move into Chicago to take control of drug territories controlled by the Black Gangster Disciples. This led to a spate of shootings whose victims included not just the members of the rival gangs, but also police officers and hundreds of innocent bystanders.

Drug sales and distribution are perhaps the most harmful type of crime carried on by street gangs. These gangs have developed connections in Mexico and Latin America that enable them to import large quantities of heroin and cocaine, which finds its way into American neighborhoods and schools. For example, in Chicago the Latin Kings reportedly smuggle large amounts of cocaine from Peru and Colombia through Mexico. The Kings may also have a direct link with the violent Medellín drug cartel in Colombia.

Another gang that has been involved in drug trafficking is Mara Salvatrucha, also known as MS-13. Mara Salvatrucha, which means "Forever Salvador," was started by a group of Salvadoran rebels during the civil war that raged in that country during the 1980s. MS-13 currently operates in major cities throughout the United States. The gang continues to take advantage of its roots, buying hand grenades and rifles in El Salvador, where they sell for far less and are much easier to acquire than in the United States. In addition to being involved in the sale of cocaine, marijuana, and heroin, Mara Salvatrucha members—identifiable by their MS-13 tattoos—also engage in burglary, carjacking, extortion, and murder. The international reach of the gang is evidenced by its means of financing some of its drug purchases: selling, in Latin America, cars stolen in the United States.

Another powerful gang whose members originally came from the ranks of Hispanics (primarily Mexicans and Chicanos) and whose criminal tentacles extend a long way is the 18th Street gang. Reportedly the largest gang in Los Angeles County, its membership is estimated at 20,000 individuals. And even in the ultraviolent world of street gangs, 18th Street has carved out a reputation for brutality. In 1997, for example, one of the gang members was sentenced to death in California for the murder of two men in a hotel during a drug deal. According to the prosecution, Frank Kalil Becerra killed Herman Jackson and James Harding following a disagreement over the sale of cocaine. The victims were tied together and strangled with electrical cords. Deputy District Attorney Elizabeth Ratinoff said that "the manner in which these killings occurred . . . is one of the worst homicides I've ever seen." She added that Becerra "is definitely one of the worst [criminals] that I have personally seen."

In addition to dealing drugs, 18th Street gang members run protection rackets, collecting money from street vendors, store owners, and other businesses in their neighborhoods. In 1994, for example, the Los Angeles County District Attorney's Office reported that it was pursuing 18th Street gang members involved in the murders of 30 businesspeople who had refused to pay protection.

During the 1990s, the 18th Street gang branched out from California to states such as Washington, Oregon, Idaho, Nevada, Arizona, New Mexico, Texas, Nebraska, Iowa, and Georgia. The gang includes many illegal immigrants from Mexico and Central America, but some 18th Street sets include African Americans, Asians, Caucasians, and Native

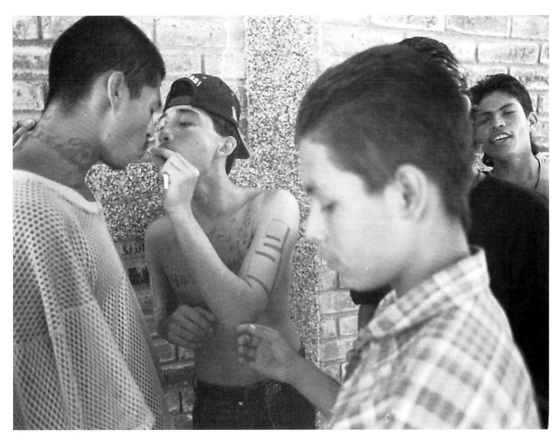

Americans. Members tattoo themselves with the number 18 or the Roman numeral XVIII. They usually wear brown or black pants with a white T-shirt.

This gang is sometimes called the Children's Army because it recruits members from elementary and middle schools. These children are indoctrinated into the gang and told that if they leave, they or their families will be killed. One mother of a gang member explained that "a boss from 18th Street calls my son and tells him what to do." She added that the members of this gang "are more ruthless, commit more murders, deal more drugs" than the people in other gangs. In an interview, her son, who had the number 18 tattooed on his forehead, admitted, "I cannot avoid associations with other 18th Street

Members of Mara Salvatrucha, also known as MS-13, hang out and smoke marijuana. Originating in El Salvador, MS-13 came to the United States during the 1980s with refugees fleeing the Central American nation's civil war. The gang has since taken root in major U.S. cities.

gang members because they call me all the time, and if I don't go with them, they will say . . . there is only one way out, and that's in a body bag."

According to social workers, law enforcement experts, and gangbangers alike, this is a relatively common story. If the experience of "jumping in"— which typically requires a beating at the hands of other gang members and commission of a violent crime—is somewhat intimidating, the prospect of "jumping out" can be truly frightening. Many hard-core gangbangers take an extremely dim view of comrades who want to abandon the gang life, and their threats of physical harm or even death are anything but empty.

In addition to their seemingly limitless propensity for violence, contemporary street gangs have authorities concerned for another reason: more and more seem to be developing direct ties to adult organized crime groups, and some have diversified into legitimate businessses, a technique the adult crime groups pioneered to launder the money gained from their illegal activities. Consider, for example, the case of the youth gang called El Rukns. Organized in Chicago in the mid-1960s, El Rukns eventually allied itself with a local businessman named Noah Robinson, who helped the gang make connections with a New York heroin dealer. Soon the gang began selling heroin in Chicago. Some of the money from the drug trade was used to start legitimate businesses, including a restaurant. The gang was also hired to kill a witness in a murder case. These are the same types of activities that are carried on by crime families that form the Italian Mafia.

Studies also show that Asian youth gangs, especially Chinese gangs, are tied to adult organized crime. These gangs were started in the 1960s by Chinese students who dropped out of school. The gangs were involved in a variety of illegal activities,

including drug sales, robbery, protection, and prostitution. Young gang members were also actively recruited into tongs—secret Chinese merchant societies (not all of which were linked to gangs and crime) formed in the 19th century in the United States to preserve cultural identity. The gang leaders acted as liaisons between the gang members and the criminal tongs. The members eventually went

The meeting place of El Rukns, a Chicago youth gang that evolved into a powerful criminal organization, largely through the distribution of heroin. Across the country, several other gangs have made similar transitions.

through an initiation ceremony to join the tongs, who kept the gangs under their control and used them to commit crimes.

No community can consider itself safe from the criminal activity of gangs. They infiltrate neighborhoods and schools, bringing fear and violence wherever they appear. Urban areas bear the brunt of gang-related crime because poor economic conditions in many inner-city neighborhoods are one of the primary reasons for young people to join gangs. During the 1980s, however, more and more gangs also began to form in the suburbs of major cities. In the beginning, these gangs were separate from gangs in the cities, but by the 1990s, urban gangs had begun forming affiliates in suburban areas. These affiliates formed for several reasons. Primarily, youth whose families had moved from the city to a suburb felt isolated from their peers and wanted to have a sense of belonging to a group. But urban gangs also began to see the suburbs as ripe new territory for their drug trade.

Why would a young person from a more affluent suburban family want to join an urban street gang? Some may be attracted to gangs for the same reason many youths in urban areas join: the breakdown of the family. For his book *Suburban Gangs*, author Dan Korem interviewed kids from the suburbs who had joined street gangs. Many reported feeling very angry when their parents divorced. Some replaced their broken family with the "family" provided by a gang. Physical abuse by a parent—a problem that knows no socioeconomic boundaries—was another factor that drove some suburban kids to seek protection as well as a sense of power by joining a gang. (Studies of violent young people, including those who have committed shootings in schools, have shown that many of them suffered physical abuse at the hands of a parent or other adult.)

Korem also points out that gangs are likely to appeal to kids for whom there is no adult at home to care for them or protect them. And gang leaders are well aware of this. As Korem relates, they often tell potential recruits: "Don't worry. We'll take care of you. We understand you. We'll be your family." Korem explains that "approximately 75% of the gang youths I have interviewed responded that they have no protector at all. They want permanence, not the anxiety of not knowing who will take care of them. They want to know that they are important to others, not the isolation brought on when families explode apart."

Unlucky
Neighbors

The job of an elementary-school principal is not supposed to be dangerous. But one principal, who lived in a small eastern city a few blocks from her school, found herself in the middle of a gang war. Two rival street gangs were fighting over the neighborhood where the principal lived, and she was afraid to leave her house after dark. Many of her students weren't allowed to play outside after school. When classes ended on Fridays, most stayed inside until they returned to school on Monday morning. Their parents were afraid that they might become victims of gang violence.

All over the country, street gangs have taken a huge toll—and not just on other gangbangers or on the innocent victims of gang-related crime. Gang

Members of the Diamond Street gang in Los Angeles sit in front of a graffiti-filled wall marking their turf. The presence of a gang in the neighborhood can have a host of negative consequences for residents.

activity produces a host of *indirect* victims as well: people who constantly live in fear for their lives, or the lives of their children and loved ones, simply because they reside in an area where violent gang-bangers operate. Gangs can traumatize, and eventually destroy, entire neighborhoods merely by their presence. In Chicago during the late 1990s, for example, the school system hired adults to escort children to school because they were too frightened of gang violence to walk the streets by themselves. According to the Chicago Police Department, more than 130 street gangs operate throughout the city. During the 1990s, these gangs were responsible for an average of more than 100 homicides annually. Unfortunately, many of the victims were innocent bystanders caught in the line of fire when rival gangs were fighting for turf or settling scores.

One Chicago resident, D'Ivory Gordon, explained her experience this way: "When I walk out my door, these guys are out there. . . . They watch you. . . . They know where you live. They know what time you leave, what time you come home. I am afraid of them."

A similar situation prevails in Los Angeles. "No neighborhood is safe anymore," explains Sergeant Wes McBride of the Los Angeles County Sheriff's Department. While violent crime committed by gangs is down in L.A., the size of gangs continues to grow, at an annual rate of almost 7 percent. Authorities estimate that there are almost 20,000 gang members in Los Angeles County alone.

Sociologist and street-gang expert Lewis Yablonsky calls South Central Los Angeles, where many violent drug gangs do business, a "nightmare landscape inhabited by marauding thugs. Innocent citizens living in the area are held hostage in their home by nightly violence, and innocent people out on the streets late at night too often wind up as victims."

An article in the *Los Angeles Times* described one Los Angeles neighborhood where residents are terrorized by rival gangs. "Life on the block means being constantly on the alert," the article explained. "One 20-year-old man who grew up on the block and still lives there has developed a survival tactic. Whenever an unfamiliar car drives by, he gets ready to hit the ground. 'If a car passes, I just get low. My friend's father got caught in a cross-fire a couple of years ago.' "

Most law-abiding citizens would love nothing more than to see the gangs leave their neighborhoods. Unfortunately, while many residents of gang-infested neighborhoods know about gangbangers' criminal activities, aiding the police or the justice system can be a risky proposition. In Pomona, California, the fate of a 14-year-old boy named Eduardo Samaniego clearly demonstrated this fact. Samaniego witnessed a gang murder in his neighborhood. Although 14 other residents had also seen the murder, most were too scared to testify. The boy bravely agreed to appear in court, but he never had the opportunity. He was murdered by gang members in an alley a short distance from his home.

The threat of gang violence keeps many citizens from testifying against gangbangers. According to a report by the U.S. House of Representatives Subcommittee on Crime, intimidation of witnesses is a fact of life across the country in cities as diverse as Los Angeles, Des Moines, and Washington, D.C. In New York, a drug gang murdered a local resident, then cut off his head and began kicking it around the streets. This was enough to frighten other people in the neighborhood into refusing to cooperate with police in solving this murder or other homicides allegedly committed by the gang.

Even if the police are successful in capturing a gang member and he is sentenced to prison, innocent

A man walks near a housing project in Washington, D.C., where residents said that gang members were intimidating them into keeping silent about gang activity in the neighborhood. Obtaining testimony against gang members has been a perennial problem for prosecutors.

citizens still report that they do not feel safe. Even from behind bars, gang leaders still direct their soldiers to inflict violence on anyone who might have testified against them. And when these leaders are released from prison, they generally continue their violent ways.

One reason for the widespread gang violence, according to Yablonsky, is the ease with which gang members can obtain weapons. Money from illegal drug sales finances the purchase of assault rifles, Uzis, and semiautomatics. And the availability of weapons has made it possible for these gangsters to carry out what is widely regarded as their signature crime: the drive-by shooting.

William B. Saunders, an expert on gang violence, notes that the drive-by became particularly popular among gangs in Southern California for an obvious reason: there is very little public transportation in the area and gang members, like other residents, have to rely on automobiles to get around. In the past, gangs had often settled disputes with rivals through rumbles. Though these melees between gangbangers armed with knives and clubs could easily turn lethal, the introduction of guns made the rumble downright suicidal. Gradually, the drive-by became seen as a more practical, and effective, way of dealing with rivals.

Drive-bys may occur for a variety of reasons. In some cases, gangs are simply struggling over the same piece of turf. One gang may want to control it to sell drugs or extort money from local shop owners. Drive-bys may also simply be a way for new gang members to prove themselves. New gangbangers can achieve status by demonstrating that they have the nerve to commit a drive-by shooting. In some instances, a gang leader may order a shooting and ambitious Wannabes carry out the crime. The drive-bys then become part of the gang's history, and the gangbangers who commit them are considered heroes. They brag about their "bravery" and win the respect of their peers.

Of course, innocent victims may find themselves in the wrong place at the wrong time when the bullets start flying. But their fate seems to have very little impact on the gangbangers. "They will readily defend themselves by pointing out they were not *trying* to harm innocents, but that is one of the unfortunate side effects of gang warfare—just like any other warfare," Saunders explains.

Some drive-bys constitute preemptive strikes—a way of inflicting injury on a rival gang before they have a chance to do the same. Of course, in the world of gangbanging, such an attack itself demands retaliation, and the cycle of intergang violence can be endless. Sometimes drive-by shooters target a specific individual who has committed a particular offense against the shooters' gang. But just as frequently, any member of a rival gang is fair game.

Parties held by rival gangs are favorite targets of gangbangers. Usually, these parties are large gatherings of gang members, so the shooters can easily find targets. In addition, the victims may be high on drugs or alcohol and unable to quickly run for cover or return fire. But the shooters might just as easily pick any place where their rivals are likely to be found. This might include a parking lot known to be a popular hangout, a gang member's house, or a park where rival gang members are known to congregate.

In Venice, California, the Shoreline Crips gang committed more than 20 shootings of rival gang members in a single year. These included not only drive-bys but also "walk-up" or point-blank murders. Authorities believe the premeditated killings were designed to protect the Shoreline Crips' drug territory.

As noted earlier, while such lethal violence may be primarily directed at other gangbangers, innocent residents of the neighborhoods where it occurs pay a steep toll as well. And to the extent that such violence is related to the use and sale of drugs, the problem of gangs in neighborhoods is at its core largely a drug problem. In his book *The Youth Gang Problem*, Irving Spergel points out that gang members may have become more involved in drug dealing as a result of changing economic conditions during the 1970s. Low-skilled jobs began to disappear as the American economy became more high-tech. Urban

Police in Louisville, Kentucky, examine the scene of a drive-by shooting believed to be gang related. A 12-year-old girl was killed as she slept on a couch, and a neighbor was wounded in the hail of bullets.

kids with a limited education, who used to be qualified for low-skilled employment in manufacturing, now found themselves with fewer job opportunities. Consequently, drug dealing began to seem like an attractive alternative.

Studies from the 1980s showed that the number of gangbangers involved in drug dealing was seven times higher than among non-gang-affiliated youth.

By the 1980s, police departments in small and large cities also began to report more extensive drug *use* by gang members as well; the proportion of drug-abusing gangbangers may reach 70 percent. This is significant because drug use is associated with increased criminality.

Despite their seven-times-higher rate of involvement in drug dealing—and despite the prominent role that the sale of illegal drugs plays in the activities of many gangs—it would be a mistake to conclude that the majority of gangbangers are significant players in the drug trade. In fact, only an extremely small percentage are.

The reason for this, according to gang expert Irving Spergel, is that street gangs have a "fluid, unstable, emotional character [that] is not suited to a rational drug organization." The illegal drug trade is a multibillion-dollar industry whose requirements for success include not simply ruthlessness, but also sophistication and business savvy. Most individual gangbangers lack the knowledge, skills, and temperament necessary to become major players in the illegal drug industry; likewise, the vast majority of street gangs lack the necessary sophistication. Thus, drug distribution is typically controlled by large organized crime groups, which may employ members of street gangs as dealers, lookouts, and enforcers.

Of course, exceptions exist. Some street gangs have been able to transform themselves into major powers in the illegal drug trade. A report by the U.S. General Accounting Office explains, for example, that in the 1970s "black gangs began dealing heavily in marijuana, LSD, and PCP, and the inter-gang violence began to escalate for control of drug markets. In the early 1980s, the gangs began selling crack cocaine. Within a matter of years, the lucrative crack market changed the black gangs from traditional neighborhood street gangs to extremely violent groups operating from coast to coast." Hispanic gangs in Los Angeles and Chicago, as well as Chinese youth gangs in New York City, are also involved in drug trafficking.

Although many experts believe that the drug trade has greatly exacerbated the violent tendencies of street gangs, without drugs these gangs would still commit acts of violence—against one another and innocent citizens. For gangbangers violence is simply a way of life.

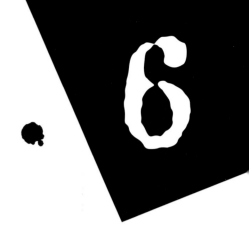

GETTING TOUGH WITH GANGS

Gang violence presents a huge challenge for law enforcement officials across the country, and the sheer magnitude of the problem demands attention. In Los Angeles County, for example, gangs committed approximately 40 percent of all murders during the 1990s.

In the face of that level of violence, many communities throughout the country—often aided by federal law enforcement officials—have adopted a get-tough approach to dealing with gangs. In Los Angeles, local police officers joined agents from the FBI and the Bureau of Alcohol, Tobacco and Firearms (ATF) on a special antigang task force. Using wiretaps to listen in while gang members discussed their illegal activities, making available additional money to pay informants, and taking extra steps to protect witnesses, the task force was able to gather an impressive amount of evidence.

As a result, the task force made more than 2,000

A police tactical squad raids a gang house. Because of the huge amount of crime they commit, street gangs have become a high-priority target of law enforcement agencies and the criminal justice system.

gang arrests between 1992 and 1995. Approximately half of those arrested stood accused of violent crimes. One gang, the Eight Trey Gangster Crips, had controlled neighborhoods in South Central Los Angeles. Police estimated that this gang was responsible for 80 percent of the violent crimes committed in the area.

In Austin, Texas, police started a special Gang Suppression Unit in 1994. Its primary role is to investigate violent crime by focusing on neighborhoods with a high level of gang activity. Austin police maintain a computerized system that tracks gang members and their crimes. "The gang unit plays a support role for beat officers," says assistant chief Michael McDonald. "If you have situations out of hand in an area, and routine patrol operations can't adequately respond, then our gang unit's role is to work with the community and officers to stabilize the situation."

In Boston, city police, working together with federal officials, have greatly reduced juvenile homicides and gang violence. At the beginning of the 1990s, gang violence had become so bad that police commissioner Paul Evans worried that Boston might "cease to be a viable city." Out of desperation, Boston police joined with the ATF to stop the flow of guns finding their way into the hands of gangbangers. Part of the solution lay in a computerized system that the ATF uses to enable it to examine the records of gun dealers. Agents noted that one dealer in Mississippi was selling a large quantity of guns to a college student, who brought them into Boston and, it turned out, then sold them to gang members at a profit. After an investigation, police arrested the student and shut off this source of firearms.

But it wasn't just law enforcement that teamed up to counter the gangs. A special task force composed of police and Harvard University experts researched the activities of gangs and concluded that most of the violence committed by Boston gang members was attributable not to the drug business, but to power struggles between rival gangs for the control of turf. As a result, Boston law enforcement officials initiated Operation Ceasefire, an attempt to bring the warring gangs together to end the violence. In addition to these attempts at mediation, prosecutors fought violent gang-bangers in court, using tough federal laws that imposed strict sentences on repeat offenders. In one case, a gang member named Freddie Cardoza was arrested for having in his possession a single bullet. Though in itself that offense would carry no jail time, Cardoza, who had a record of violent crimes, was convicted under a federal law called the Armed Career Criminal Act (ACCA) and sentenced to 19 years in prison.

Law enforcement officials are also using another federal law, the Racketeer Influenced Corrupt Organizations Act, or RICO, to deal with gangs. Passed in 1970, RICO was designed to combat criminal organizations such as the Mafia, but the act has more recently been applied to street gangs. In basic terms, under RICO an individual gang member can be convicted of a crime if prosecutors can prove that he belongs to the gang that committed it; prosecutors do not have to provide convincing evidence that the individual gang member actually committed the crime himself.

Using RICO, police have been able to arrest and convict gang members far more easily than in the past. RICO has been used against Asian gangs on the East and West Coasts, the Bottoms Boys gang in Louisiana, and the Bloods and Crips in Omaha, Nebraska. In Michigan, the Safe Streets Violent Crime Task Force used RICO to prosecute the Home Invaders, a gang that had burglarized more than 100 houses in the Detroit area.

Few Americans would complain about the above law enforcement and criminal justice measures. A threat as serious as gangs requires a robust response. But in the zeal to stop gang-related crime and violence, various jurisdictions have taken steps that are some-what more problematic.

In Chicago in the early 1990s, for example, city officials passed an antiloitering law giving police the power to arrest individuals who were "in any one place with no apparent purpose." Police officers used the law to approach young people suspected of being gang members who were loitering—that is, standing around in a park, parking lot, or street corner doing nothing. Between 1992 and 1995, police issued tens of thousands of orders to disperse and made approximately 45,000 arrests under the statute. The police activity, it might reasonably be argued, probably prevented a number of crimes that gang members would have committed had they been allowed to loiter unmolested: selling drugs, for example, or vandalizing property—perhaps even robbing passersby or planning drive-by shootings. Plus, by removing the suspected gangbangers from the area, police allowed law-abiding citizens to move about their neighborhoods and enjoy their parks without fear of being victimized by gang members. Certainly no one could argue with that goal.

However well intentioned the authorities may have been in implementing it, civil libertarians took a dim view of Chicago's antiloitering law. Young people were targeted for police scrutiny—some would say harass-ment—merely because they were suspected of being gang members. There is no doubt that many *were* gang members, but others undoubtedly were not—and were doing nothing except hanging out with their friends or standing in front of their houses. A Chicago man named Luis Gutierrez contends that he and two friends were simply talking on the street when police arrested them. (A judge later dismissed the charges.) "It was really upsetting," Gutierrez said. "A lot of people they arrested were innocent kids who don't need to see a jail."

And even if a kid standing around on a street corner were, in fact, a gang member, that fact alone would not

be grounds for an arrest. In the United States, the law punishes only conduct; it does not punish mere membership in a group. If the gang member weren't engaged in proscribed conduct at the time, then he would have as much right to be there as anyone else.

Of course, the statute itself made standing around, or loitering, the proscribed conduct. And while in general the courts have upheld the right of jurisdictions to enact laws treating minors differently from adults (by, for example, imposing curfews or prohibiting truancy), freedom of assembly—the ability to congregate peacefully in a public place when and with whom you choose—is a right guaranteed to *all* citizens under the First Amendment to the U.S. Constitution. Loitering may be prohibited, but just what distinguishes loitering from being in a certain place for an acceptable reason becomes subject to interpretation—and, as a practical

Luis Gutierrez (shown here) was arrested under Chicago's controversial antiloitering law, which was designed to combat gang activity but ran afoul of the Constitution.

matter, to interpretation by police on the beat.

In turn, police discretion became a major concern of civil libertarians who objected to Chicago's anti-loitering statute. Were police applying the same standards for different groups of young people who seemed to be loitering? Or would they, for instance, treat differently a group of white kids sitting on a curb in an affluent neighborhood and a group of minority kids doing the same thing in a poor neighborhood? Most of the arrests were of African Americans and Latinos, suggesting that the law was indeed being applied unfairly. And the consequences for the minority youths—many of whom already had educational and socioeconomic disadvantages—could be serious. As Rita Fry, a public defender in Cook County, later remarked, "These arrests left thousands of innocents with a police record, a record that can make it more difficult to seek employ-ment, to obtain credit or to access certain benefits."

Based on these and other concerns, the American Civil Liberties Union (ACLU), a legal group that takes cases defending individual rights against government encroachment, challenged Chicago's antiloitering law. In 1995 an appellate court found the law unconstitu-tional, a ruling upheld by the Illinois Supreme Court two years later. But Chicago appealed the decision to the U.S. Supreme Court, which heard arguments in the case, known as *City of Chicago v. Jesus Morales, et al.,* in December 1998. The following June, the Supreme Court upheld the decisions of the lower courts, ruling that the antiloitering statute was indeed unconstitutional.

That ruling may affect other statutes aimed at combating gang activity. For example, during the 1980s some communities in California began to compile databases with the names of young people suspected of being gang members. These databases expanded to many California cities, including Los Angeles, Newport Beach, and Huntington Beach. During the 1990s, California governor Pete Wilson

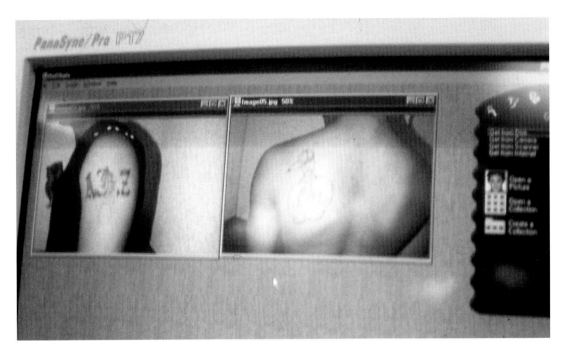

developed a statewide gang-tracking system called CalGang, which lists the names of more than 250,000 young people—many of them gathered from the lists of suspected gang members compiled by California communities.

According to one 15-year-old girl, she and her friends were waiting to use a pay phone when police approached and accused them of being in the area to buy drugs. Their pictures were taken and their names added to a gang database. "We weren't affiliated with any gang," said the girl. Indeed, as it turned out, all were honor students in high school who later went to college. Believing that the police had violated their rights, the young women contacted the ACLU.

The ACLU won the case and the women received $85,000 in damages. More important, the law was changed: police must have "reasonable suspicion" that an individual they want to photograph is a criminal, and they must obtain consent from the person before taking the picture.

Images from a law enforcement database of suspected gang members. A number of jurisdictions have set up similar databases, and critics wonder whether some youths are being unfairly stigmatized.

Despite the legal setback, other California communities have decided to go after suspected gang members with tough laws. In San Jose, for example, individuals suspected of being gang members are prohibited from "standing, sitting, walking, driving, gathering, or appearing anywhere in public view" with anyone else who might belong to a gang. Suspected gang members are also prohibited from carrying "glass bottles, rocks, bricks, chains, tire irons, screwdrivers, hammers, crowbars, bumper jacks, razor blades, razors, sling shots [and] marbles." Similar laws have been passed in Los Angeles, Oakland, Burbank, Pasadena, and Long Beach. According to one Los Angeles prosecutor, "From our experience, it has had a tremendous . . . effect on gangs. It provides breathing space for the neighborhoods to get out from under the constant intimidation caused by the gangs in the area."

In Santa Monica, California, a judge ruled that members of the Crips could be prevented from engaging in "precriminal" activities in neighborhoods that are considered part of the gang's turf. Such activities include carrying legal weapons or ammunition, and going outside after 10 P.M. Crips are also prohibited from hanging out with other gang members. Similar action was taken against the Langdon Street gang in San Fernando Valley. A judge prohibited members from being on the streets after 9 P.M. and from talking to each other by two-way radios. These devices are often used by gang members to warn one another that police might be in the area during a drug sale. Prosecutor James Hahn defended the judge's decision because, he said, the gang was "a cancer which has survived more that 15 years of law enforcement efforts to [remove] it from the community."

In 1987, Los Angeles asked a judge to prevent members of the Playboy Gangster Crips from wearing gang colors, owning guns, hanging around with other gang members, having paint that might be used for graffiti, or going out at night. Law enforcement officials

GANG FREE
ZONE

GANGS

THE VEHICLES OF
GANG MEMBERS ARE
SUBJECT TO SEIZURE
AND IMPOUNDMENT

TOWN ORDINANCE

CICERO
67400

SPEED
LIMIT
30

In 1999 Cicero, Illinois, posted street signs alerting people to a town ordinance permitting police to seize the vehicles of known gang members. The American Civil Liberties Union promptly sued, claiming that the measure was unconstitutional.

believed that such a tough approach was necessary to prevent gang activity.

But the ACLU and other groups contend that these types of laws violate the civil liberties of ordinary citizens, especially their rights under the First Amendment. More court challenges are inevitable.

If laws designed specifically to target gangbangers have raised constitutional concerns, and if many such laws may ultimately be overturned, the police have other weapons in their arsenal for combating gang activity. For example, many departments have simply devoted more officers to antigang efforts or even created special squads for that purpose. The Los Angeles Police Department's Special Enforcement Team logged

70 percent more gangbanger arrests in 2000 than it had the previous year. Speaking of one neighborhood where this effort substantially curtailed gang activity, an LAPD officer remarked, "You won't go down there now and see groups standing around intimidating people. They congregate and, boom, we are there."

In Los Angeles and in other cities across the country, police units are also paying special attention to taking gang leaders off the streets. Experts estimate that older, hard-core members are responsible for about 70 percent of a gang's violent criminal activity. Targeting them thus can have a significant impact on serious gang-related crime.

In some cases, however, the mandate to do something about America's gang problem seems to have led some police officers to go outside the law. One such case involved three LAPD officers who patrolled an area where illegal drug sales were rampant and where frequent turf wars broke out between the MS-13 and 18th Street gangs. The officers were convicted of framing gang members for various crimes. (It should be noted, however, that in recent years the LAPD has been plagued by a variety of scandals, and the actions of the three antigang officers may be part of a more general pattern of police misconduct rather than a specific result of the effort to curb gang crimes.)

In any event, reactions to the police convictions were mixed. Some citizens applauded the convictions, believing they would encourage much-needed reforms in the LAPD. But many people who lived in the neighborhood in question expressed concern that the police would not be as tough on gang violence in the future. "If it wasn't for the police, this place would be nothing but lawlessness," one resident said in an interview. "I can't talk bad about the cops because imagine what it would be like around here without them."

The police, of course, will never solve the gang problem on their own. In fact, how the criminal justice system deals with gangbangers probably will always play just as important a role as any initiatives law enforcement might undertake. In general, the recent trend in American criminal justice has been to punish violent juvenile offenders harshly—a trend that fits public opinion. In the past, youths under the age of 18 who broke the law wound up in special juvenile courts, where for the most part they received more lenient treatment than did adults who committed similar offenses. When punishment involved incarceration, the sentence was served at a special juvenile facility (and the offender was typically released no later than his or her 18th or 21st birthday, regardless of the crime). Today, while the majority of young offenders still go through the juvenile justice system, many states have passed laws allowing juveniles accused of violent crimes to be tried in adult courts and, if convicted, to receive the same punishment as adults. The threshold age for being tried as an adult varies from state to state. In Wisconsin, for example, a child as young as 10 who is accused of murder can be tried as an adult; in Oregon, the age is 15.

While these laws are part of a general effort to "get tough" on violent juveniles, not an attempt to specifically target gangbangers, many criminal justice officials see them as a good tool for getting gang members off the streets for a long time. The 1999 case of four minors who belonged to a street gang known as the Slick 50s serves as a good example. Seventeen-year-olds Jesse Grist, Steven Crader, and Kurtis Pinedo and 16-year-old Joshua Riazi were charged with attempted murder for stabbing someone at a party. Tried as adults and convicted, the gang members all received long prison sentences: Grist, 17 years; the other three, 15 years.

While many Americans support efforts to get violent gangbangers like the Slick 50s off the streets for as long as possible, advocates for these youths believe there is a better way to deal with the nation's gang problem.

Second Chances

J ames Wilson joined a gang while he was still in junior high. Like other gang members, James committed a variety of crimes, some fairly minor (for example, shoplifting) and some quite serious (such as participating in a drive-by shooting). James was finally arrested when police broke up a gang fight in a small park.

Each year almost 3 million young people under the age of 18 are arrested, and many of them belong to gangs. Of the 3 million, only 100,000 are put behind bars—of whom some 8,000 do time in adult prisons.

By far the most common form of punishment handed down to juveniles is some form of probation.

Inmates at the Shutter Creek Correctional Institution boot camp march as a drill instructor barks out orders. Authorities hope that the rigorous discipline of boot camps, modeled after military basic training, will instill in young gangbangers qualities that will enable them to turn away from the gang life.

James, for example, found himself under the supervision of a probation officer. Although he was allowed to live at home, James was supposed to check in with his probation officer regularly. The other conditions of James's probation stated that he must refrain from all contact with members of his former gang, stay drug-free and never carry a weapon, and attend classes at high school regularly. Failure to comply with those conditions could land James back in juvenile court—and possibly expose him to incarceration. It was up to James's probation officer to monitor his progress.

Probation officers frequently set up treatment programs for juveniles who may need different types of assistance. This may include drug treatment, tutoring in school, or career counseling. Unfortunately, many probation officers have enormous caseloads and cannot spend a great deal of time checking to make sure that all of the juveniles they supervise are abiding by all the terms of their probation. Often, even the most conscientious of probation officers can only follow up when there are clear warning signs that a youth may be getting into trouble again—for example, if the youth fails to check in at the required time or if the probation officer receives a report from school officials that the youth has been truant. Under such circumstances, many young people are bound to slip through the cracks.

James Wilson was one of these people. He returned to his gang and resumed his criminal activities. Recidivism, or a return to criminality, is what happens to the majority of juvenile offenders on probation, not just those who are gang members. One way that law enforcement officials have tried to deal with the problem of recidivism is through stricter monitoring. Some gang members on probation are placed under what is called intensive supervision. Under this type of program, a probation officer is given a much smaller caseload. Juveniles in the officer's care are required to check in several times each week. Intensive supervision may also include a strict curfew, which requires the juvenile offender to remain at home unless he or she is attending school or working at a part-time job. In addition, the offender may be required to wear an electronic ankle bracelet that enables the authorities to ensure that the juvenile is complying with the curfew.

Some gang members who have committed serious offenses may be placed in day treatment programs. These programs required them to attend special centers during the day where they receive counseling and drug treatment, as well as help with their academic courses and career guidance.

Another approach that has been used to treat young offenders is the boot camp, which is modeled after the basic-training programs that military recruits undergo. The offenders are required to sleep in barracks, wake up early every morning, wear uniforms, take long marches and do other strenuous exercises, and follow all the orders barked out by their frequently intimidating adult instructors, who function like army drill sergeants. The idea is to break down and remold the young offenders' personalities, replacing destructive and antisocial patterns of thought and behavior with self-discipline, a sense of self-worth, and respect for authority.

The purpose of all these programs is to help gang members and other offenders leave behind their criminal lives and reform themselves. Unfortunately, it can't be said that any of the approaches has been overwhelmingly successful. A majority of violent juvenile offenders return to a life of crime, whether they are placed on probation, sent to boot camps, or put behind bars in correctional centers.

As a result, many experts have begun looking for ways to lure young people away from gangs *before* they commit serious crimes and enter the juvenile justice system. In his book *Suburban Gangs*, Dan

Latino gang members turn to view a display of legal, health, and educational information during a gang truce rally. Experts believe that effective antigang efforts must offer socially acceptable alternatives for success to the young, marginalized people who typically join gangs.

Korem points out that there are several reasons youths leave gangs—whether they are located in the suburbs or the inner cities—and exploiting these reasons may hold promise for antigang programs. Fear, for example, can be a strong motivator. A young gangbanger who sees friends die suddenly and violently may be afraid enough for his own safety to want to leave. Then, too, many young people join gangs in order to find a sense of security or belonging that's missing in their own broken families. Some become disillusioned when they discover that the gang really doesn't provide these things, or that gang leaders are exploiting them. In some cases a young person's family may even overcome its problems and begin to function effectively again, so he no longer needs a gang. And a few gang members may even become bored with the gang's activities and find other interests, such as a job or a career in the armed forces. (Of course, the most antisocial, hard-core members of a gang are unlikely to voluntarily leave for any reason.)

All of these factors have come into play in successful efforts to turn around gang members and lure them away from violent crime. In Washington, D.C., for example, a 12-year-old boy named Darryl Dayan Hall was brutally shot to death while walking home from school early in 1997. The murder so shocked two rival gangs in the area that they agreed to meet with a group called the Alliance of Concerned Men. Alliance members had also belonged to gangs when they were younger, so they knew how to talk the language of the streets. In conversations about the turf warfare, both gangs admitted that they "couldn't remember why it started," but all agreed that it had gone on long enough.

The Alliance helped gang members to get jobs, such as cleaning up and removing graffiti from walls for the D.C. Housing Authority. In addition, the Alliance directed gang members toward apprentice-ship programs in business or toward returning to high school to get their diplomas. According to one police officer, crime in the area has gone down by more than 50 percent. "They are totally changed young men," the officer said.

Isis Sapp-Grant founded one of the most violent female gangs in Brooklyn, New York. Called the Deceptinettes, it was associated with a male gang called the Decepticons. "I realized that there were a

Rico Rush of the Alliance of Concerned Men hugs former gang member Eric Reavis after the organization brokered a "peace treaty" between two warring gangs in Washington, D.C.

lot of violent kids at school," she said. "But if I acted crazy, they kept their distance. And I found that the crazier I acted, the more respect I got." Sapp-Grant remembers beating up and robbing people on the subway. Indeed, the Deceptinettes gained such a reputation that, according to Sapp-Grant, "we could close down any school by calling the school office and telling them [we] were coming. People were that scared." She recalls also the murder of one boy who was beaten up by the Deceptinettes, then shot by members of the Decepticons.

Sapp-Grant explains that she joined the gang because she felt that "no one cared about me and so

I wasn't going to care about them." Raised by a single mother who didn't spend much time with her, the girl grew up with a deep well of anger and resentment. As a member of the Deceptinettes, she seemed like the kind of hard-core, extremely antisocial gangbanger who would die an early, violent death or spend a large part of her life in prison. But her first arrest, and a week in jail, changed her outlook dramatically. Returning to the streets, she found herself frightened by the thought of her future as a gang member. Would she end up dead, paralyzed, or addicted to drugs like many of her friends?

When her mother told Isis that she didn't want these things to happen to her, Isis recognized that she still cared. Isis also received extra help and guidance from several teachers, and she managed to graduate from high school and go on to college. Eventually she earned a master's degree in social work.

Today she works with young people, especially girls, who are at risk of becoming gang members. "If you're going to tempt these kids away from the thrill of violence—and violence can be an incredible high—you have to make them understand that somebody cares about them, that they are not invisible or power-less, that their life means something," she says.

In Boston, the Reverend Eugene Rivers has used the same approach in dealing with kids who live in Dorchester, one of the city's poorest sections. Rivers runs Baker House, a refuge for young people who are at risk of joining gangs or who may already be gang-bangers. In 1992 a terrible assault occurred at the Morning Star Baptist Church. Gang members chased a young man into the church and stabbed him during a funeral service. A group of Boston churches decided that the time had come to help pull kids out of gangs. Church leaders met with Rivers and decided to work with the police to bring an end to gang violence.

Rivers enlisted volunteers to work with him at

Baker House, which helps more than 1,000 young people each year. His message is that religious values must replace the values of the street. Only the church, Rivers believes, can provide a true family for young people who may not have one at home. And only an institution like Baker House can help young people find the security that a gang can never provide. Rivers himself was a gang member as a youth. But an evangelical minister took an interest in him, saved him from the gang, and led him into the religious community. Now he is trying to do something similar for other kids.

The police in Boston, having concluded that "get tough" policies wouldn't solve the gang problem, decided to work closely with Rivers. As one officer put it, "We realized that preachers have tremendous credibility as leaders in the community and that having them working with us out in the streets would have a powerful impact." Now gang members who have been arrested meet not just with probation officers, but with local ministers as well. Plus, police officers and members of the clergy visit at-risk young people before they have joined gangs. Observers believe that the program has great promise, and gang violence in Boston has plummeted.

In Chicago the Back of the Yards section, a high-crime area, is being transformed by the teamwork of local gangs and neighborhood homeowners. Many of the young people who live in the Back of the Yards area are high school dropouts, highly susceptible to the lure of gangs.

Although most residents were fearful of gang violence, a group of adult mentors decided that something could be done to change the neighborhood environment. Together with parents, teenagers (some of whom belong to gangs), and representatives from the Chicago Department of Human Services, they formed the Neighborhood Youth Committee. Adults

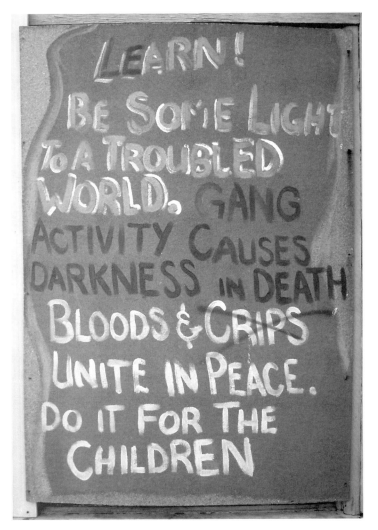

A sign pleading for peace between the Bloods and the Crips graphically demonstrates just how intractable the gang problem may be: "Crips" has been crossed out, presumably by a Blood.

on the committee made an effort to talk with gang-bangers and find out about them as individuals. The result was an increase in mutual understanding between gang members and the rest of the residents in the neighborhood. Adults finally understood the anger and frustration experienced by the kids. Many had turned to a gang for acceptance after failing in school, seeing no hope of finding a job, and believing that they weren't wanted or appreciated by their families or community.

The committee began to offer alternatives to these youth, encouraging the young people to finish high school and offering scholarships to those who were accepted at college. The committee also implemented a job-training program and organized special events, such as dances and talent shows, for young people. A recent study credits the committee's efforts for a significant reduction in violence in the Back of the Yards section.

Programs that involve gang members have also been implemented in other communities. In Providence, Rhode Island, for example, the police department's gang unit started a six-team football league that includes rival gangs. Providence's police chief explained the rationale: "If these gang members release their energy in a positive way on the football field, they'll be too tired to fight each other on the street at night."

The federal government has also earmarked funds for community programs to combat gangs and to help gangbangers who want to leave the gang life. Cities like Chicago have received grants of from $200,000 to $400,000 for new initiatives. "Kids want to find a way to get out of the gangs, but they don't know how," says author and sociologist Irving Spergel.

In the Chicago program, several youths were redirected onto a new path. One, a gang leader, had been seriously injured in a shooting. "My boys left me lying there bleeding," he said in anger. With help from a team that included social workers and police, he began studying for a high school diploma and was placed in a part-time job. Experts believe that programs like this, which not only address the emotional needs of troubled youths but also give them concrete, socially acceptable opportunities for economic advancement, offer the best hope for reducing gang membership and gang violence.

Of course, no one is naive enough to believe that any government or private program will totally eliminate the problem of street gangs, which have, after all, existed since the earliest days of the United States. The gang life continues to hold a strong attraction for many vulnerable young people, particularly those who are failing in school, have dim prospects for getting a decent job, and don't have a happy and emotionally secure family to fall back on. As long as there are young people in that situation, America will probably always face the problem of street gangs.

Bibliography

Beiser, Vince. "Boyz on the Rez." *The New Republic*, March 10, 2000, p. 15.

Cohen, Warren. "The Windy City's tough tack on street gangs." *U.S. News & World Report*, on line, December 14, 1998.

Garza, Mariel. "Gang Bang." *Reason*, October 1999, p. 15.

"Going after gangs." *Current Events*, May 6, 1996, p. 1.

Kinnear, Karen. *Gangs*. Santa Barbara, Calif.: ABC-CLIO, 1996.

Korem, Dan. *Suburban Gangs*. Richardson, Tex.: International Focus Press, 1994.

Leland, John and Claudia Kalb. "Savior of the streets." *Newsweek*, June 1, 1998, p. 20.

Maggi, Laura. "Tough Neighborhood Turns Around as Ex-Gang Members Wise Up." *Nation's Cities Weekly*, June 7, 1999, p. 7.

McGovern, Timothy and Bruce Wellems. "The survival of an inner-city Chicago community." *Parks & Recreation*, August 1997, p. 56.

Sanders, William. *Gangbangs and Drive-Bys*. New York: Aldine De Gruyter, 1994.

Sapp-Grant, Isis, and Rosemarie Robotham. "Gang girl: the transformation of Isis Sapp-Grant." *Essence*, August 1998, p. 74.

Siegal, Nina. "Ganging up on civil liberties." *The Progressive*, October 1997, p. 28.

Sikes, Gini. "Girls in the hood." *Teen Magazine*, March 1997, p. 50.

Spergel, Irving. *The Youth Gang Crime Problem.* New York: Oxford, 1995.

Tyre, Peg. "New York turns up the heat on Crips, Bloods." CNN Interactive, August 27, 1997.

Valdez, Al. "18th Street." National Alliance of Gang Investigators Associations. *http://www.nagia.org/18th street.htm*, 2000.

Vistica, Gregory. "'Gangstas' in the Ranks." *Newsweek*, July 24, 1995, p. 48.

Witkin, Gordon. "Swift and certain punishment: how to keep young toughs from committing violent acts." *U.S. News & World Report*, December 29, 1997, p. 67.

Yablonsky, Lewis. *Gangsters.* New York: New York University Press, 1997.

Websites
House of Representatives Subcommittee on Crime. "Gang-Related Witness Intimidation and Retaliation," June 17, 1997. *http://commdocs.house.gov/* committee.judicary/

Index

Index

Index

Index

RICHARD WORTH has 30 years of experience as a writer, trainer, and video producer. He has written more than 25 books. Many of his books are for young adults, on topics that include family living, foreign affairs, biography, and history. He has also written an eight-part radio series on New York mayor Fiorello LaGuardia, which aired on National Public Radio. He presents writing and public speaking seminars for corporate executives.

AUSTIN SARAT is William Nelson Cromwell Professor of Jurisprudence and Political Science at Amherst College, where he also chairs the Department of Law, Jurisprudence and Social Thought. Professor Sarat is the author or editor of 23 books and numerous scholarly articles. Among his books are *Law's Violence, Sitting in Judgment: Sentencing the White Collar Criminal*, and *Justice and Injustice in Law and Legal Theory*. He has received many academic awards and held several prestigious fellowships. He is President of the Law & Society Association and Chair of the Working Group on Law, Culture and the Humanities. In addition, he is a nationally recognized teacher and educator whose teaching has been featured in the *New York Times*, on the *Today* show, and on National Public Radio's *Fresh Air*.

Picture Credits